The Art of Pregnancy Photography

By Hector M. Melendez

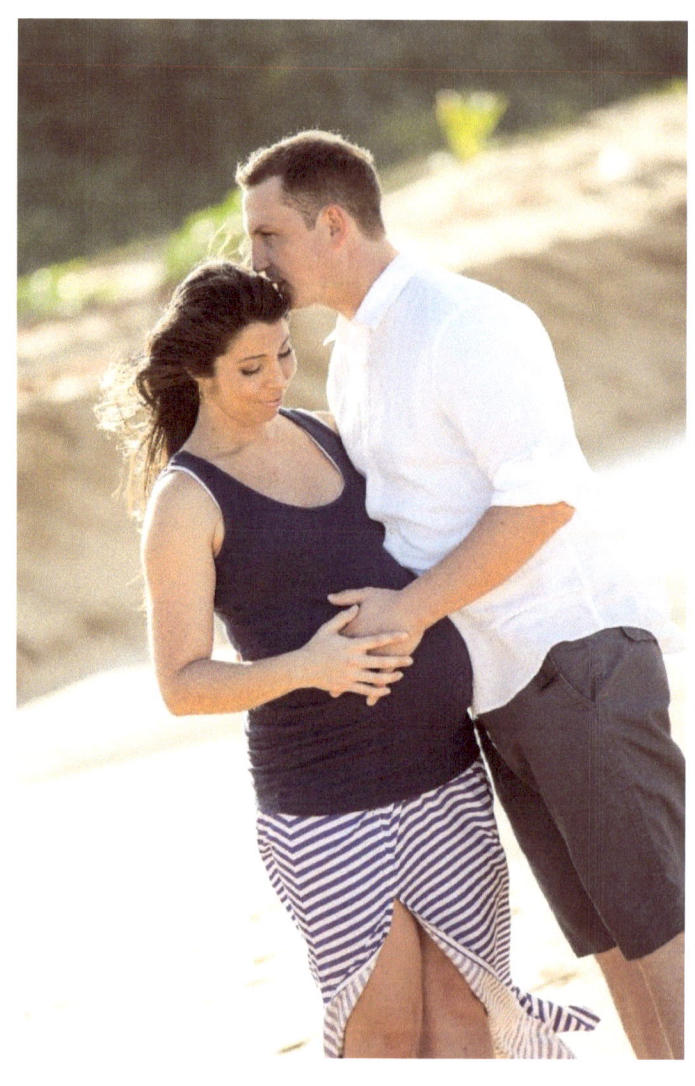

Copyright © 2020 Moicam Photography

All rights reserved.

CONTENTS

Title Page

Introduction

Posing

Romanticism

Clothing

Light

Tips to take great photos

Equipment

Contingency Planning

Editing

Final Product

INTRODUCTION

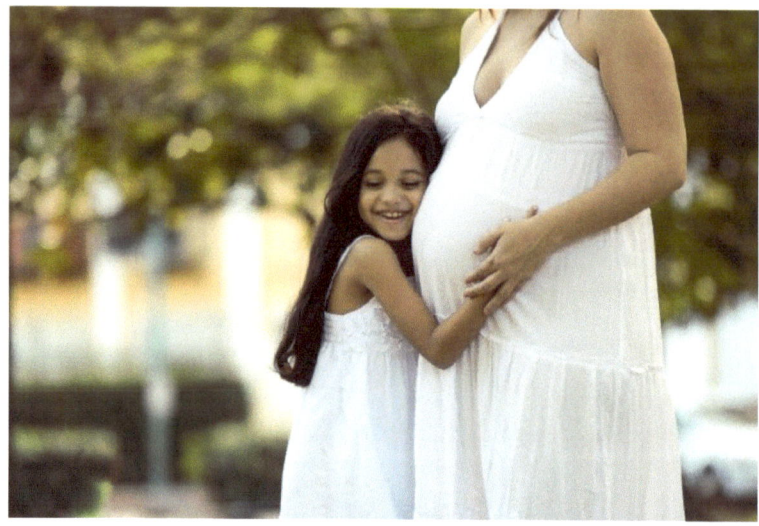

Pregnancy is an incredibly special time in human life. It means that the arrival of a new member to the family is approaching. Many couples choose to hire a professional photographer to capture special images after the sixth month of pregnancy. In my experience pregnancy sessions are a very intimate moment of the couple, so they prefer that the photos be taken in places such as a photographic studio for privacy or outdoors in places with few people around.

This is what helps the relaxation of the subjects in this type of sessions, which helps us to obtain natural expressions. I live on a tropical island, which helps me to have outdoor sessions throughout the year. All my pregnancy sessions have been in botanical gardens and beaches in the island of Puerto Rico as you will see in the images in this book. If you want to learn how to take beautiful pictures of pregnancy, you will enjoy reading this book.

POSING

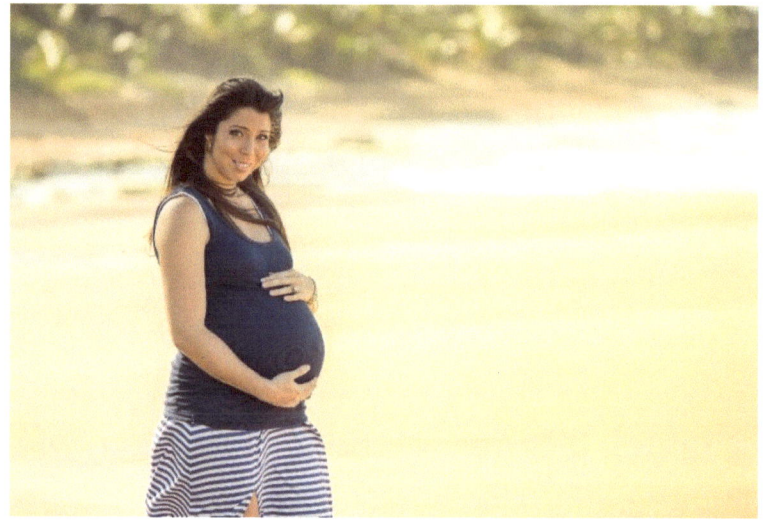

To have a successful session, posing our subjects is extremely important. You need to help the couple to get into some basic poses, and from there continue to vary. Sometimes they will do their own poses without realizing it.

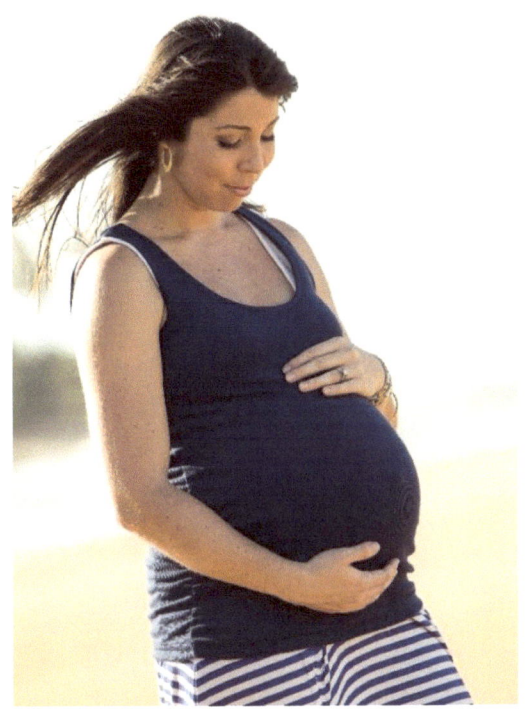

When the mother to be is alone, the hand of the arm closest to the camera should be below the belly while the other arm should rest above as shown in this image. The hands need to look relaxed. The mother to be can look to her belly, then to her front, and then to the camera.

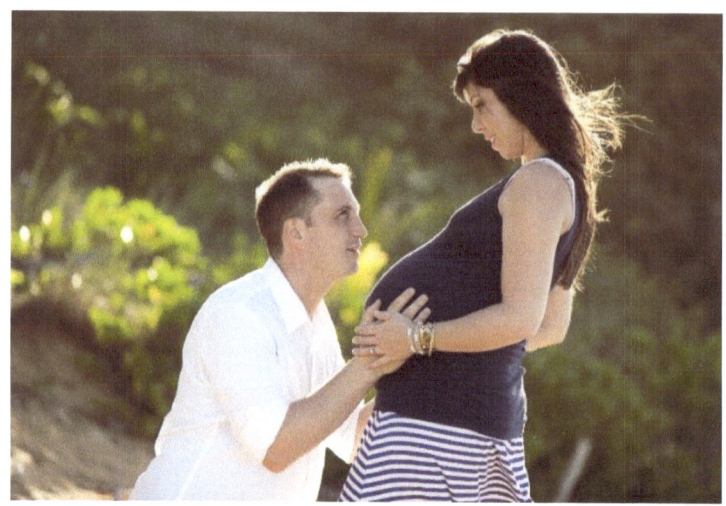

The pose of the father to be kneeling before the belly of the mother to be is special. In this image he looks into her eyes. It is especially important to guide the couple to vary the poses. In this way we will have more varied images when delivering the final product.

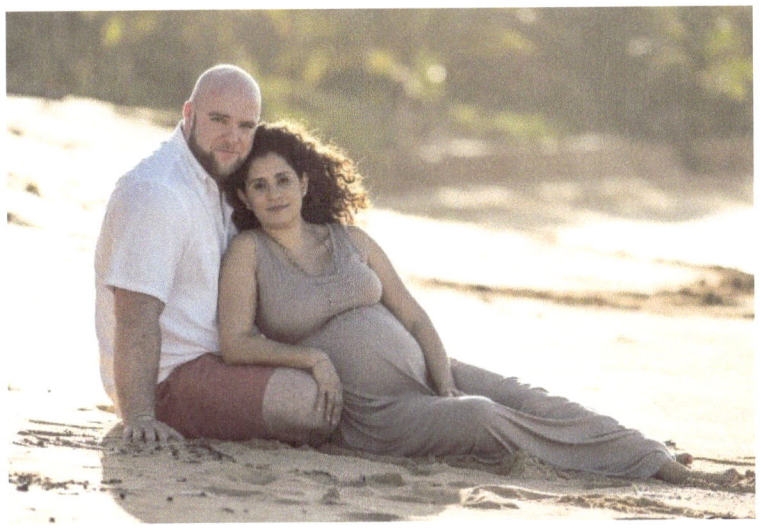

The pose in which the couple is sitting in the ground also can look exceptionally good as you can see in this image.

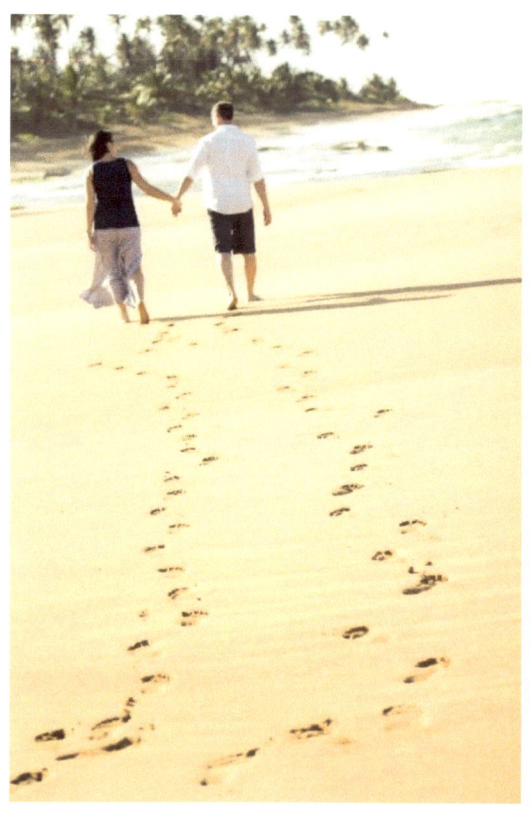

If you have the opportunity you can tell the couple to take a walk. In this image I noticed the footprints in the sand. I did a tilt of the camera and achieve one of the most special photos of this session.

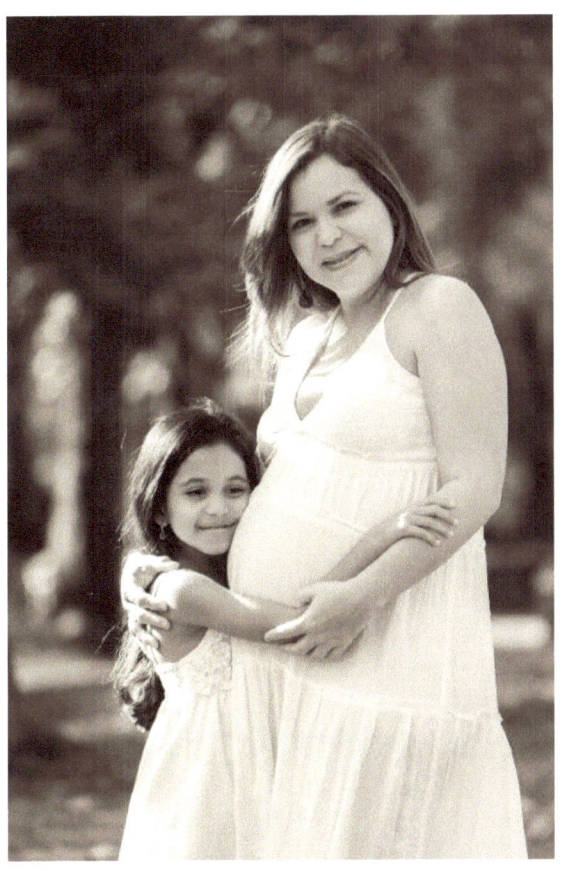

Future big brothers and sisters are welcome in the sessions. In this image the girl shows love for her mother and is waiting for her younger brother to born.

ROMANTICISM

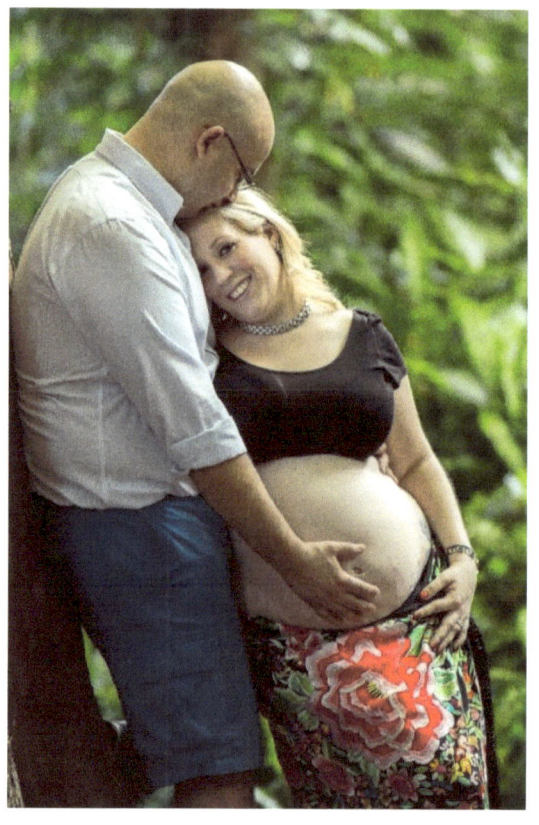

When the father to be is in the session, it is important to show romance between the couple, since the unborn baby is product of their love. I pose the couple, tell them to talk about fun things and then I go a bit far to avoid intimidation. From there I hear nothing, but with the power of my lens it seems that I am remarkably close. I wait for special moments. In this pose the mother to be is in a romantic pose with her husband, and for a short moment she looks to the camera, which makes this image incredibly special.

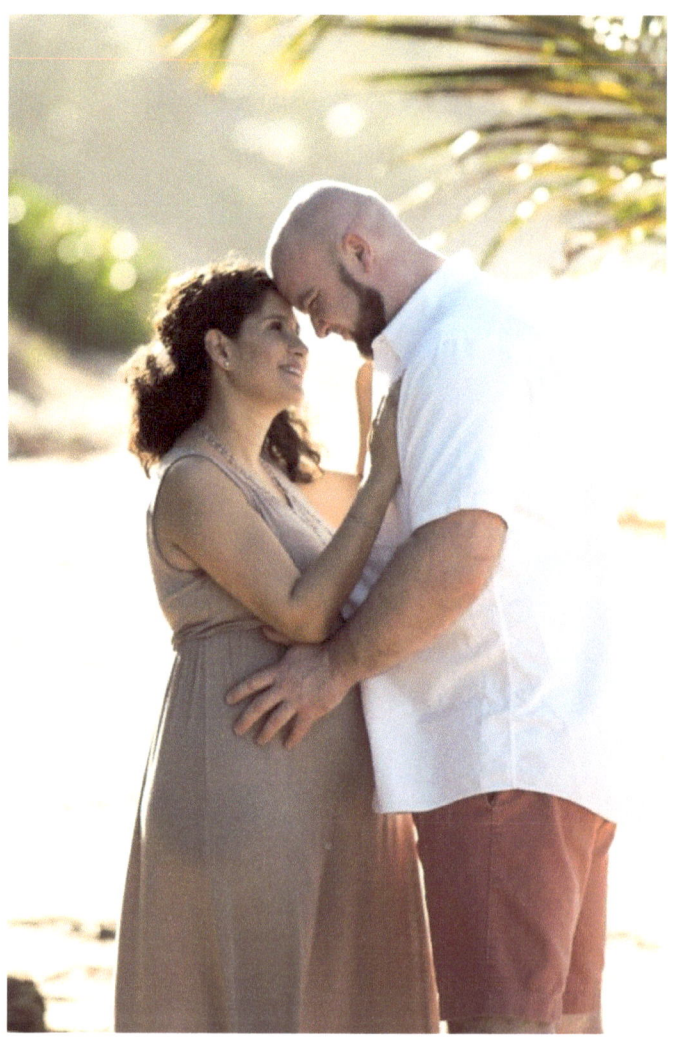

The parents to be will create their own poses sometimes, as in this image, so you must always be prepared.

CLOTHING

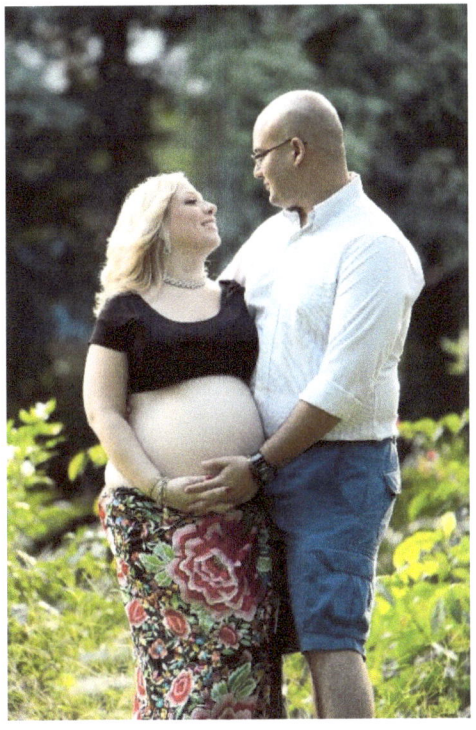

I prefer solid colors. Fresh and comfortable clothes are the best. But sometimes the couple decides. In this session the mother to be decided to wear a colorful skirt and have her belly naked.

LIGHT

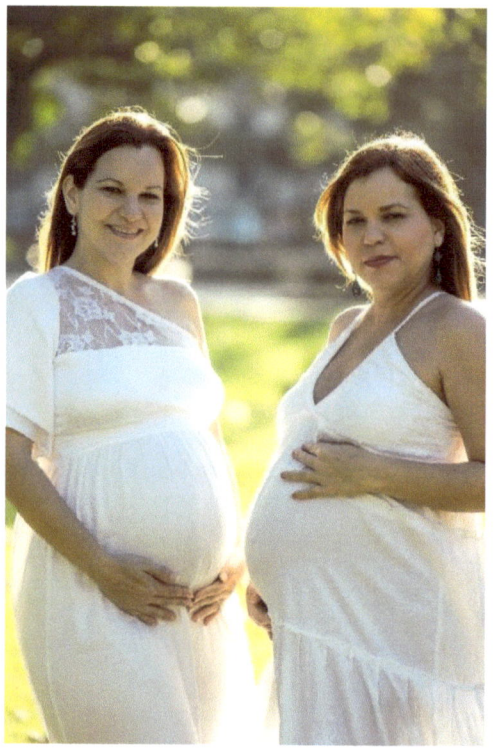

In my sessions I always work with natural light unless a little fill flash is necessary. Always remember to do your sessions in the afternoon. Try to start three hours before sunset. The more the sun falls, the warmer the colors. This way we have no unwanted shadows and flat colors of the midday sun. It is important to use the light that enters between the trees to our favor. This way, when we throw the background out of focus, it can look interesting.

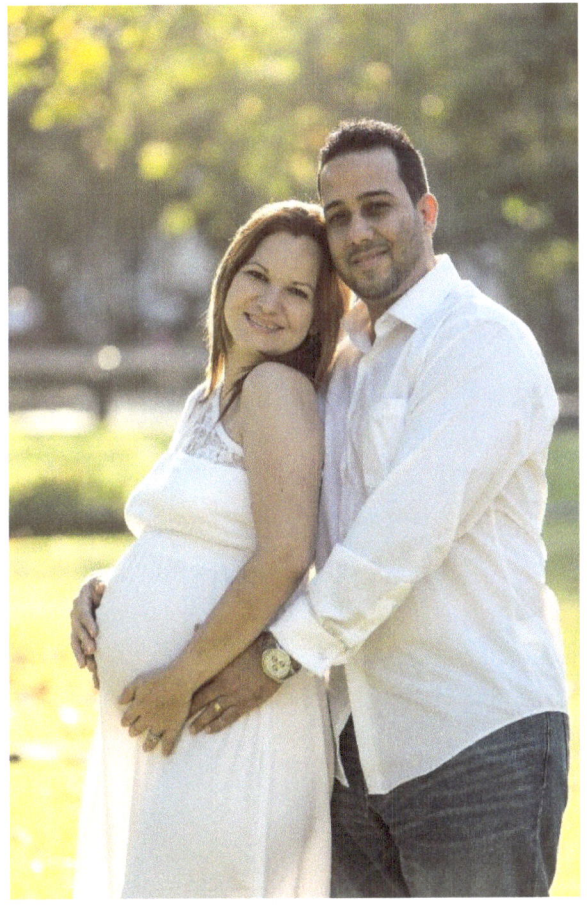

Try to position your subjects with the sun lighting their back. This way we can achieve dramatic images.

TIPS TO TAKE GREAT PHOTOS

Let us always work with the camera in burst mode. This way we try not to miss the perfect moment. We should never be worried about running out of memory. These days memory cards are quite economical. Buy memory cards with enough space and always have backup.

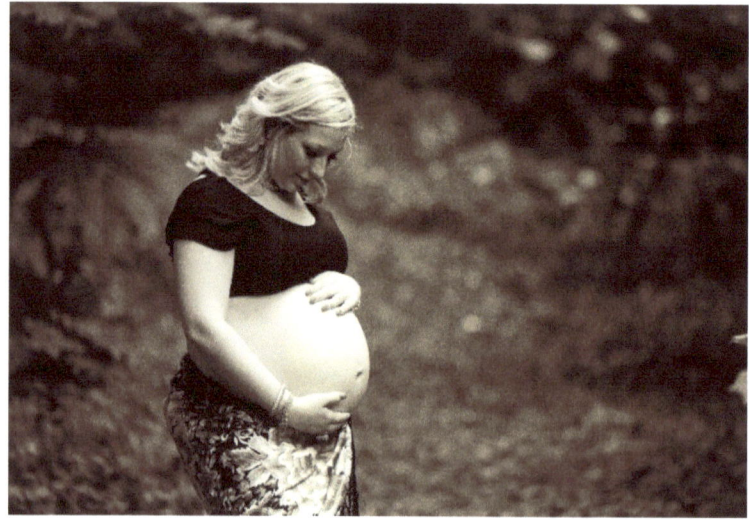

For me it is important that our images look clean. There must be the least number of objects that distract the eye of the viewer. There should be no people other than our subjects. It should appear that our subjects are alone in the photo. That is why throwing the background out of focus is important. This makes our subjects the main characters. Less is more.

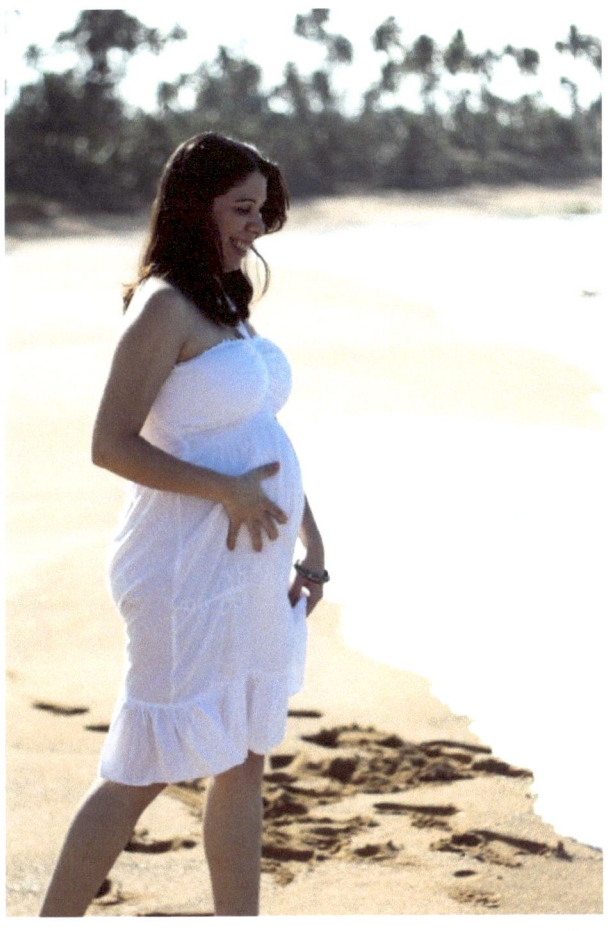

Try to take almost every image with the lens at its maximum focal length to throw the background out of focus. Use the spot meter on the camera to measure light with a neutral color, like the green of the grass.

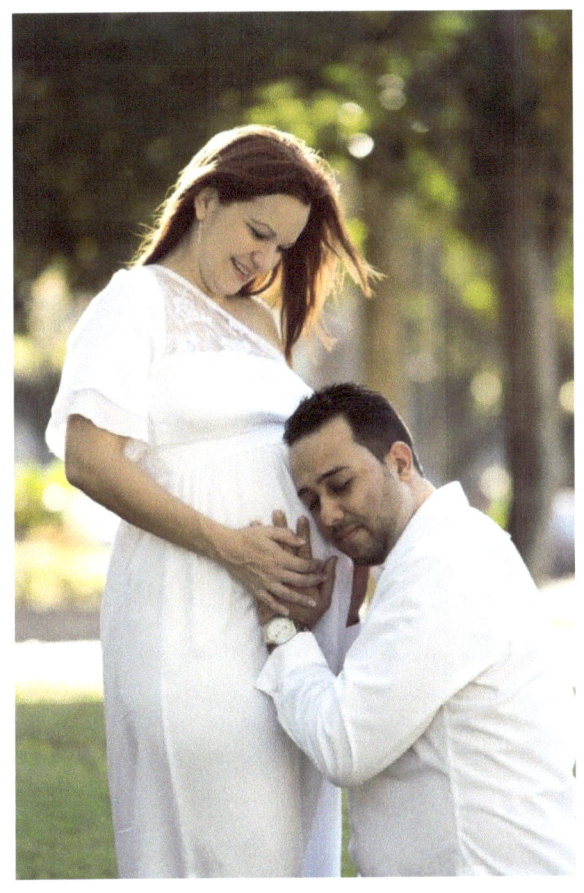

Be aware of changing light and measure again if needed. Always be prepared for the moment having both hands on the camera. Compose with your eye carefully and take the images. This way we avoid spending more time editing. Remember that cropping too much reduces image resolution.

EQUIPMENT

- Two DSLR cameras
- Super Telephoto 70-200mm (for full size sensor camera) or 50-150mm (for APS-C sensor camera) with 2.8 fixed aperture at any distance, and image stabilization
- Backup lens
- Battery grip for more energy time and better camera handling
- Two memory cards with space for at least 1,000 images each
- Lens cleaning kit
- Lens hood
- External Flash

CONTINGENCY PLANNING

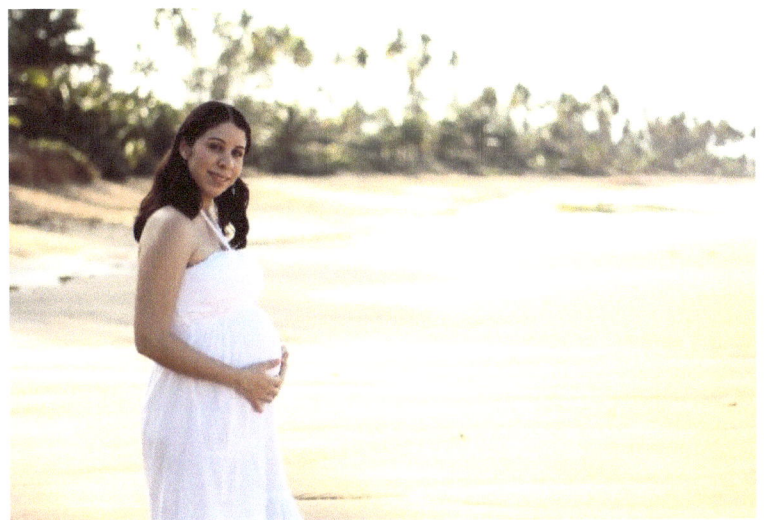

Making backup on a computer, external disk drive and in a cloud service, the same day of the session, is a must. When editing, make backup of your work at the end of the day.

This way we avoid losing our work in the event of any accident.

EDITING

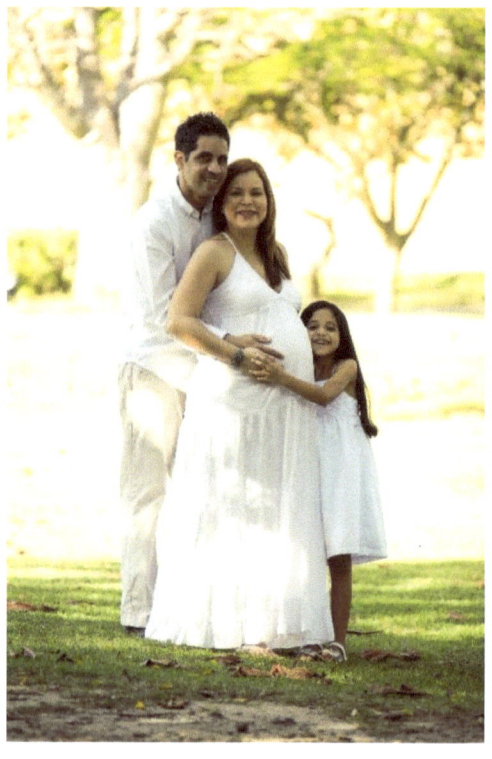

My advice is to take all our photos in RAW format. This way we will have more control when editing. We can crop, adjust white balance, raise, or lower up to two full stops in case we miss the correct exposure due to light changes, and we can adjust shadows, highlights, and colors. Photos in jpeg format are not very manageable.

Use a good desktop computer application for handling RAW photos format. After we finish editing, we convert to jpeg format for the final product.

FINAL PRODUCT

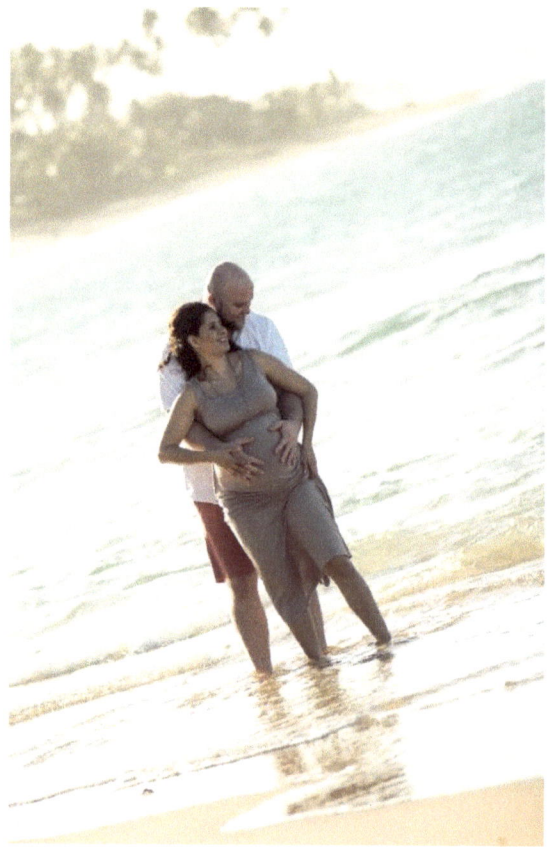

Since in my pregnancy sessions I always work with my camera in burst mode, I can end up with around 500 photos per session. Already sitting in front of my computer I start selecting the photos that artistically meet my requirements, and then

I start editing. I deliver around 35 color images with copies in black and white, in a well-presented device. On the internet we can find several photography companies that help us with interesting quality items and devices to store photos.

www.ingramcontent.com/pod-product-compliance
Lightning Source LLC
Chambersburg PA
CBHW040349220526

45473CB00009B/2827